Free Falling

Free Falling

Poems by

Bill Mayer

Cover design by Shay Culligan
Cover photograph by Bill Mayer

ISBN: 978-1-949229-76-9

Kelsay Books
Aldrich Press
www.kelsaybooks.com

For Jane,
Vaidya Priyanka, and her staff
Gioachino Franco, and the staff at Sunridge Medical

Acknowledgments

Fifteen Roads—The Translucent Guides, Wind, The Beautiful Changes, and *One Morning in San Jose* were published in Visions International #93, #96 and #98.

Also by Bill Mayer:

The Uncertainty Principle
Longing
The Deleted Family
Articulate Matter
A Truce With Fantasy

Contents

Part 1

The Beautiful Changes

The Beautiful Changes

The planes that take off from the valley are completely silent.
I count them—Ah, a *Constellation* though is best, overhead,
the four engines pushing apart the borders of the sky.
　　　　　Like an operation, the folds
of flesh opened to get at the meat, the heart,
subterranean
　　　　　　　　like the caves we built—do you remember?
　　　　　　　　　Or on North Dome, in early Spring,
that first night, an onion skin granite slab,
the snow already melted away. In my sleeping bag,
stars everywhere and then in the morning
across the valley, avalanches in the sun
while drinking tea,
　　　　　　　　the Plane trees hardly moving
in the hot air, cicadas like some mad orchestra
tuning. Living on an island where you try to love,
at least learn from the effort; five years, ten years, is not so long,
but long enough, a sighing final breath out,
into what cannot be remembered,
　　　　　　　　　　a boy drowning quietly
after the party.
　　　　　　Love is never completed; it is always
at the starting point, after thirty years,
fresh when it seems stale, otherwise repetitive,
　　　　　　　like mountains from the ridge, all the other ranges
ever continuing into the distant haze,
into the forgotten life, forgotten love, a childhood
bursting from the chrysalis of old age.

Still Sore Where They Cut into Me

How do you wake from the long, dreamless sleep,
barely able to recognize anyone,
and then forget everything
until a day later? What is this process
that reminds us of death
while so vastly different,
is dreamless as death is,
but cannot compare,
except that we do, and then
ignore as quickly as we can?
It is true the personality we love
we lose, that which makes us ourselves.
There may be some truth
in continuance, the after of our after,
but this slow waking is also divine,
precious as a bus stop is, protected
from the driving rain
in the darkening afternoon,
a temporary shelter, yes, as we go,
still shivering, on our particular way.

A Venetian Tower, an English Mystery

The Corsairs landed on the island,
quickly overcame the simple farmers,
raped the women and took some of them away.
What little resistance there was
was easily and brutally quelled.
The islanders in the tower below us,
all brothers, were completely outnumbered,
slowly starved out, and then, after first
killing their own sister
so that she would not be dishonored,
left the tower waving their arms and shouting,
and were slaughtered.

I looked at the tower every day
from my window. One day,
took a ladder down to it
and climbed up into the one opening,
about twenty feet above the ground.
There was nothing there, just rubble.
There should have been ghosts,
but they had all been scrubbed clean.
Even in moonlight, the tower was silent,
as though everything that could be said
had been said over and over again
in the violence of every subsequent age.

Nothing for us here, said the inspector, buttoning his coat.
Let's get back into town.

Shostakovich at the Elevator

You'd think the blood would know when to stop,
not spurt out of the wound into the air;
you'd think the screaming amputee could force it back,
could heal himself, say, like the miracle man
in the Australian outback who simply picked up
the hacked-off flesh and put it back onto his body, scarcely
pausing as he did so, and continued on, to the other
man's astonishment.
All anger and violence subsided, the waters calming,
reflections of stars and a late moon brilliantly mirrored
in the mountain-rimmed glacial tarn. You'd think
we would learn, however long it took. Flowers, he thought,
in the cold air, his small suitcase packed, waiting
for the thugs to take him away, his only sin a clarity,
and the refusal to pretend what others did smilingly,
and so eager to please.

Sand Dunes at Midday in Winter

Shadows of nothing
seen through a lens
a swirling
storm in repose
White and more white
silent brilliant unbearable

A small patch of hard earth
in the fold between dunes
a blossoming mesquite bush
mysteriously thriving
Kangaroo Rat trails
and hollows
Also
the track of a sidewinder
last night

The tracks of a beetle
as it traverses
the highest dune
make no noise

After you have stood
in the middle of
the Coral Pink Sand Dunes
for a time
they lose all color
and you shake your head
rub eyes baffled
and only regain it
once you have gone
back to the car
put things away
get ready to go

then

Sand dunes like sponges
collect water
so that
it is easy to climb them
early in the year
but extremely difficult
in August after
they have emptied

If you are a photographer
the wind does not
obliterate footprints
as quickly as you would wish

and it's nasty
even with a tripod
for those delicate plants
the faintest wind
your picture ruined

I will grow Sand verbena
and desert trumpets
a garden when it rains
lilac carpeting the dunes
otherwise
I will grow glass

So easy to photograph them
in the morning or late afternoon
so difficult when there
are no shadows
But that is

exactly
what I want

Someone made
a swirling maze-like circle
out of large black rocks
in a sand depression
It was still there the next year
but not the following

Birds fly over the dunes
but never land
their cries
are the perfect definition
of loneliness

Finding a tiny bit
of shade under the mesquite bush
I ate an orange
drank water
and thought of nothing

We were trying to figure out
whether the strange
five-sided block formation
was natural or man-made
My friend said it was
constructed I said not
We still don't know

By 2 pm the sun
is moving west
and it is time to go back
to our camp

45 minutes away

I am tired and sticky
the shadows are making the dunes
feminine
They are becoming
conventionally
beautiful.

Not to be dismissed of course
peering into the black
of shadow
into the beauty of line
of definition

I am content in this brightness
in this soft air and quiet
Just don't come
in summer.

Reinventing the Harpsichord

New York Intellectuals have passed me by.
West Coast Experimentalists are not interested.
How did I become a backwash in the stream?

State of the Union

On a beautiful early summer's day
the sirens are constant,
obliterating
the Baroque chamber music
on our small kitchen radio.
Oh, fortunate dead.

Halliburton

It was exhausting digging in sand under the great rock.
Perhaps we could find the Ark in the ancient passage
that led from the spring up to the Dome. Or maybe
it was somewhere else—I swam the Panama Canal,
paid my fee according to my tonnage (absurd, I know)
and then walked across the Malay Peninsula, swamps, snakes,
and God knows what else, but I did it. Like flying to Timbuktu
in the red *Flying Carpet*, and just barely recognizing the fuel tank
in the middle of that lonely desert, and so much more. Most
      of all though,
following Odysseus' journey from Troy back eventually to Ithaca.
That life thrilled me, even though I invented much of it. Still,
it was enough to transfix a small boy, lonely in his room
      in Los Angeles.
Who knows what it would make of him, or he of it?
I now question the frantic travel, not merely because it led
      to my death
trying to cross the Pacific on a Chinese Junk; rather because
      I needed
to stop somewhere, feel the earth underneath me, I a part,
      I, restless,
too much in a hurry to stop and concentrate, fall in love, now
sleeping in the water, burning to tell you how I missed
      the main thing.

Fifteen Roads—the Translucent Guides

1)

It was always easy to pretend,
and in time it became an art.
Because fantasy is one thing,
invention another.
Therefore I would languish,
never sure whether what I wanted
was a life lived in clarity,
or simply weakness emboldened
by intelligence.

2)

The little girl suddenly sees
fifteen roads branching out
from a circle, and has no idea
which one to take.
There are no landmarks anywhere,
a steeple, a silo, a familiar farm,
just the endless Kansas plain.
I think her choice matters,
though this is just a story,
a fiction to lead me to a better place.

3)

Finally the fog has cooled the afternoon;
there are trains off in the distance,
but no insects, no frogs,
the birds have gone quiet.
A stillness, an approaching storm.

The plain is a human plain,
and though we are all here,
in our houses or on the way to them,
it is like a cornfield in September,
the rattling husks reminding us
how we are failing,
how the dream has lost its moral clarity.

4)

How can this be?
The unconscious is amoral, isn't it?
Isn't that what we are told?
That we are animals without any sense of the future,
grasping and gloating, greedy and helpless—
that's what we are told. Not our dreams,
not our sweet fantasies which harm no one.
It takes courage to dream into our true selves.

5)

I was thinking of that scene where the elves are leaving,
going west in a procession. They are real, but difficult to see,
silvery in moonlight and among the great shadows of the oaks.
It is like that now; the animals are leaving, going extinct daily,
leaving our world, but without complaint, or rancor.
You can see it in their eyes, a kind of soft but wild regret.
They are preparing the way out for us, leading us
the way we have led ourselves into an earth
that will soon be uninhabitable.

I think they are telling us, however,
that it doesn't matter, that nature always survives,
even if we have failed to heed her in our own arrogance.
It is a strange kind of comfort to be so led, and forgiven.

6)

Unfortunately, there are no guides for what I want.
Even if there were, they'd be in a language I do not know,
nor could ever learn.
All morning I have been looking at clouds,
trying to find some sort of message there.
What I see is like coming over the pass
and finding still more desert off to the horizon,
just the road disappearing in the hazy distance.

7)

Even the heat in my memory begins to merge
with the other heat, the desert, or Los Angeles,
as I drive slowly along its crowded freeways,
my back soaking wet against the seat,
so that I must peel my shirt away when I get out.

8)

No, the heat I mean is Greek heat,
the *Melteme, bel tempo,* heat
of those long Summer days on Paros

when I sat on the stone porch naked,
trying to find a poem, trying
to make an order of my life,
while Jan searched for ancient marble
in the stone walls that surrounded our house.
So much heat that I'd get up, walk back
to the little cistern where we had diverted

the stream, dip a pitcher into the coolness,
and pour it slowly over my body.
But this heat was thirty-five years ago,
gone into the wisp of memory, by now
certainly inaccurate, likely a dream.

9)

Who is the person who pours water over his body?
who is the dreamer in the desert heat,
where dust devils whirl off in the distance,
dissipate, and die into the earth,
like our dreams, like our tenuous hold
on the world, in memory, on the drying of skin,
of the dust settling and the traffic
growing louder and louder in the huge city,
while I try to work, while I try to remember
what it was that brought me to these places.

10)

It is like the art of division, where,
if you do not have a starting point,
no one is divisible, nor less than whole.
Let us say that no one invented time.
We would, in essence, live forever,
because there was no way to measure
when we lived or when we died.

11)

We would roam through the jungle,
our bright smooth bodies in harmony
with the leaves, the great trunks

and rustling beasts in the dark.
There would be no fear.
Only ourselves, doing what we do.

12)

We would never ask you not to feel,
never dismiss the grief of the sufferer.
A group of young men and women
are standing, talking, dressed in costumes
of the early 20th Century. Are they angels?
Are they telling me that my true life
is outside of almost everything I know?
They are not looking my way,
and are speaking in a language I recognize
but somehow cannot understand.

13)

Everything is blurry, smeared as on a canvas,
bleeding into a phantasm of dreams.
I am moor-less, like kelp far out at sea,
but it is not my element—no fish, no sky,
nor herbal scent. No dwelling place.
The earth, the ocean—these are not mine,
nothing to be consumed, all is contaminated.
I waft among the spirits of the dead.

14)

To be old is nothing, they say.
To be unknown is a duty,
they say. It is my job
slowly to untangle the threads,

each of them, not from asceticism,
nor in denial, not as a discipline,
but having experienced, having gratitude,
and to leave them with my blessing,
and not to long for their return.

15)

We will be walking on the beach.
We will once again invent singing.
The gods will come out from the rocks,
and the trees above the shore;

they will appear by our side
and tell us there is nothing, nothing at all
that we can do which will destroy anything,
that we never have the last word,
and the nightmares will end.

Part 2

Octets

Wind

Well, Grief is not the only thing we do here.
Sometimes you just have to tie things down,
secure the edges, put up the poles, hoping they don't snap,
and somehow get yourself inside, then listen
as the wind almost flattens the tent over you.
No, you'll not get to sleep as long as it lasts:
this is an endurance test, it takes all your attention,
and right now, you're not about to meditate on transcendence.

What We're Going to Miss

Oh, fine, I thought. She's made her nest exactly where
she made it two years ago and which was destroyed by squirrels.
And now she's back, or one like her, the tiny nest looking
as though constructed of concrete, an inch and a half across,
and wonderfully hidden in the brilliant spring leaves.
Maybe this time it will work, babies and the rest.
But, damn it all, I'm leaving, won't be back for a few weeks.
This story will just have to go on without me.

The Desperation

This is how it is: The authorities are all dead. Any information
has been twisted so that the old ways no longer work, if
      they ever did.
The apples are finished. Next year won't help. It's exhausting,
but the more you scratch the surface, the more layers you find.
Perhaps that's your blessing. What will grow out of this drought?
What papers can you present to show anyone? It is beyond
what you can know. Just say to yourself: Do not ignore.
      Do not ignore.
The oyster is still pulsing, but you cannot replace the shell.

Beyond Defiance

After the long hike back from the sand dunes,
I realized I'm definitely not as strong as I was
before the operation. Though I don't feel old,
I keep getting messages. *You may listen or ignore,*
they advise, *but there are consequences.* I'm thinking,
Fine, there's always a third way. Go out, buy a truck;
use it, take care of yourself as well. Eternity is a place
where time trips, not the other way around.

Standing Still when Everything Else Is Moving

Illness brings its own perspective that cannot be seen through
until after, and then you forget. You are reduced to small things:
the comfort, or lack thereof, of sleeping in the big chair
because you cannot lie down. The room not your bedroom,
your wife on the other side of the house. Nothing seems right,
but soon becomes normal. So that, as you slowly heal,
the healthy world remains strange and brutal; the light too bright,
and you want to go back. This is one train where there is no arrival.

The Resurrection Rag

What does it matter if we come back but don't know
        we come back?
Getting rid of the ego must be some kind of substitute
thanks for coming consolation prize.
I want Jane, my friends, the wind scraping sand verbena
on desert dunes. Tasha climbing on me
and wedging herself between us as we sleep.
No transformation for me into the immortal atoms
of the world, swirling out of nothingness and regret.

The Deadly Florist

There are times when I think the purpose of flowers
is to make us hesitate in the midst of the horror of the world.
Nature will save us, we think, forgetting
just how ruthless it is in its wet grasping of tendrils,
glistening in the destruction of our gardens and our structures.
Angkor will disappear again, this time for good.
yet the heavy-scented blossoms of wisteria deceive us,
slowly, masterfully, as they feed on our hearts.

Thirty Years with One Woman

All the best authorities say that infidelity is necessary.
Why didn't Wallace Stevens run off with his secretary
and really mess up his life? It would have made him a better poet,
they say. Look at the examples: Byron, Shelley and Goethe,
Pound and Eliot. After all, the great Kings all had mistresses,
Droit du Seigneur, the male fantasy of unlimited access to women.
And even though your early life leaves little room to
          complain, still,
how could you have missed out so spectacularly well?

The Three Birches

My parents gave me three birches on my 3rd birthday.
There was a shallow circular trough around all three.
As I grew so did they. When I moved into the bedroom
at the west end of the house, their leaves shuttered the sun
in the afternoon. They gave me the sound of the wind.
Most of all, they gave me the shadows I am grateful for,
a memory, now that they have long been cut down,
which I have lived with all my adult life.

Why Do This if the Self Is Not Real?

He decides to cut off the callous skin.
At first he is cautious, fears going in too deep,
so he is very careful. But then
he builds his courage and cuts deeper,
vertically now, into the flesh, not minding
the blood. Goes down further, ignoring the pain,
trying to probe the center, if it exists,
and questioning what to do once he finds it.

Not Finished

Sun on my neck as I begin to rake the leaves
for composting. When you begin to see light
as something you can touch, you are getting somewhere.
The late July brightness helps bring me back.
The long recuperation is taking root,
and the scent of the dry leaves as I push them together
is just like new wine. Intoxicated, almost faint,
thinking maybe I'm not through with this earth after all.

The Recipe

It was simple to go to the doctor, and to the dentist;
it was simple to make life routine, rise, drink tea,
eat the same breakfast every day, go to the gym.
It was so simple, my life wrapped in a down jacket,
warm with the cold wind and blue stars outside,
the men and women prowling beyond the doors,
the boats forcing their way through sea water.
So simple to die protected and secure.

The Awkward Magnificence

It is so strange, the clumsy act we've been assigned to,
our continuance, but an act so sloppy and graceless
in which we find longing and unimaginable beauty.
Though often ruined, made ugly and distorted,
this is our inheritance, the brightly colored baton
we pass to another, unseen, whom we cannot know
or imagine, to a future improbable as science fiction,
a beauty only religion can mimic, and oppose.

No Visitors

My father is somewhere in the huge cemetery in Los Angeles,
And my mother 150 miles away in a small plot in Santa Maria.
My father is in there whole, my mother in ashes.
I keep wondering if they are pissed with me for putting them
so far apart. Though she seemed not to have cared.
My father was the love of her life, I think the same for him.
The ghosts though, are nowhere near their remains. It is difficult
to track them. And it is true, I've never visited either.

Fall Harvest

I am waiting for the waxwings to come.
The pyracantha bush is heavy with red berries,
which means it is about time. They seem to know
exactly when the brilliant berries are ripe. One day,
I tasted one; not a good idea. It happens only once,
and they come in a rush, their faint, high pitched, wheezing calls
bring dozens more with a rush of wings. They are drunk
with pleasure, and when they leave, the bush is bare.

Greek Isle

How to imagine the island forested, the bare hills no longer,
as once all these islands were covered by a skin of trees?
The nude mountains I know, whose structure, unembarrassed,
is open to the sky, once were dark, matted with growth,
thick with underbrush, fern and brooks from springs above.
It is as though in our frantic blindness we wished the earth
to become a desert, we wished to abolish green, to be as we are:
naked, defenseless, raped even, and, weirdly, proud.

The There

On the ridge nothing grew. I could look in one direction
and see bare mountain, grey and red and yellow rock;
in another the great glaring white valley playa
with the bigger mountains behind, and snow, and a white sky.
No humans. There was only shape, and form, to be deciphered,
maybe photographed, or not. I just stood there and listened,
listened to my own heart beating, to what was inside my heart,
and then, faintly, the small inside that, maybe a beginning,
       maybe not.

Improper Riddle without an Answer,
Yosemite Falls

Surely we were designed to know everything we need.
Surely there is, inside us, a place we have foolishly blocked,
that the animals know and never question or doubt.
How can we be equipped with so much, arriving to the top
of the waterfall plunging almost two thousand feet below,
the great booming coming back to us like a distant gong,
but still unable to accept, still utterly empty, and turning away,
seeking reassurance instead from the worst possible sources?

Paradox World

I would make a box of water, hold its sides with just my hands,
and with utmost care preserve perfect right angles.
Let it gleaming stand alone on the kitchen table. You have to be
especially careful, so that nothing spills, so that order
       is maintained.
It doesn't matter that the heart revolts, imperious dictator of
       what is possible,
or that the mind is pleased, mastering the impossible.
It only matters that the man, standing in the corner, his hat
       pulled low
over his eyes, would reach out to destroy it, but is frozen in time.

Reincarnation

One day, I discover that I remember everything
from before. But how do I tell my new parents?
They'd just put me away. That's no fun.
Better to say nothing, start over, and go through
the whole damn thing again, keep secret my knowing
until, in time, once again, I forget.
From then on, it's all fragments, a palimpsest
that makes no sense, except it must.

Souls of the Birds

It astonishes me how much they are like us,
or that Descartes could so easily dismiss them, certain
they had no souls and were not to be considered.
But the birds chirp noisily in the bare branches of our tree.
It has rained heavily during the night and the wind is up,
They're fine, though, and the hummingbirds are at the feeders
as usual. They don't mind the wind or the cold.
Learning, learning, to discover most everyone is wrong.

Working at My Past

Those tiny butterflies, or maybe moths that congregate
on the lantana bush, I have known since childhood,
the long proboscis probing into the scent of the plant.
I was remembering how I captured them, dove into the pool
and let them float up back into the air and, fortunately,
fly off almost every time. Thinking of my childhood cruelty
with shame, still, after so many years, gathering,
darkening everything—a penance, not entirely understood.

Hermes Again

Another bird has flown into my office, terrified at first,
beating wings against the windows, then slowly settling,
resigned as I hold her gently and show her the way out.
There are messengers everywhere, fluttering and crawling,
even the painful welt on my knee that mysteriously arrives
and slowly departs. Pain is almost sweet when my ankle
refuses to let me walk. So I hobble into the bathroom,
astonished to find doors opening everywhere, even as I resist.

Hammering against the Wall

The obsidian I found high on the slopes of Mauna Kea
was meant to be an adze, but split apart in the making,
and then was tossed away. For me it serves as a doorstop
and a memory. But the living is inside it;
the mystery remains. Why should we stop there?
Why not bring everyone into the light? Who makes the rules?
Granted, some will not be happy. But that is hardly the point,
is it? all of us jostling around like tadpoles in a glass jar.

What We Don't Know, We Know

My Grandmother said once there is something faster than the
        speed of light:
the speed of thought. It was her way to explain the physical world
was not the only world. Is pulling away, therefore,
an acquiescence to the inevitable or the introduction to
        a new phase?
They say Shelley stayed the arm of his friend on the *Lago di Como*
as the storm worsened and a larger boat passed, offering help.
He wanted, we think, to find out what death was like,
something new, untested. And he was curious.

The Challenge

The great redwoods outside this beautiful retreat
slide into blue haze. Is it night coming, or morning?
The scent of the trees is comforting, like a blanket.
And how fortunate we are to hear nothing other than crickets
and the sound of fire. Fire in the wind, great fire of cleansing
and compassion. We will let the night sounds protect us
and secure our childhood. We have begun this difficult process
of mourning and praise. There is no going back.

Finding Some Way

The air is filthy from forests and thousands of homes burning.
The chemistry released from the destroyed houses drifts around us
and is frightening. Therefore, I cannot take my usual walks.
The cats though, are more affectionate than usual, needing
       to be inside
and with us on our beds. And yes, the news tells us one
       ghastly thing
after another, but somehow we manage. It is contrary in
       human nature
to abandon hope. This is the most admirable quality we have.
Joy is possible. This is the exercise I still must learn to practice.

Vaughan-Williams on the Hill above
Ecoivres, 1916

We went up the steep rise behind the mess
at sunset, Below us was a landscape like a Corot painting.
As though the war, the dead, the dying and severely wounded
we had earlier picked up under shelling was time and miles away.
I could hear a girl singing a Brittany folksong, as the sun dropped
under the hill. I thought of George, already dead, and the others
to follow. How could I make music out of this? And why
would anyone be in the least interested to hear it?

The Cure

That was the easy part. But there are more urgent matters.
For instance, why scientific discoveries rarely solve anything.
Or why the best people sail off to the west in delicate ships and,
except for a brief note left at the pier, are never heard from again,
saying how difficult it was, but they had fun trying.
Every answer deserves a serious question, but how strange it is
that the important ones are never even discussed. You'd think
being human was the simplest thing in the world until you tried it.

Part 3

Desert Songs

Desert Songs for the End of Time

1)

There is an exile who has traveled nowhere, lives still in his home,
but nonetheless has discovered it no longer exists.
There is an evenness, a smoothing out, as concrete covers stones,
as home begins to burn, to ignite the mind while history fades.
I mean one may search for fifty years and find wonderful things,
yet it remains secret—is the sky unchangeable? is its blue,
seen through our eyes, a hook that we may ride, as on a lift,
riding over the great pines and desert canyons?
What was so clear thirty years ago is today burnt, the ashes
softly drifting down, over our lidded eyes, rubble still smoking,
a dim recollection of a past that never was but will ever continue.
They say sound leaves the earth in waves, travels forever
through space. It will never arrive, but also will never cease,
until, folded upon itself, will perhaps return ever so briefly
on its eternal way. This is what we are like. Like. Like.
As though such a word could describe anything perfect.

This Summer's days passed so smoothly, like a boat
on faintly rippled water. *Can you tell*, asked the man
as we stood high above the *Mosel* over and among the vineyards,
which way the river flows? And we looked at the oxbows below
and could not answer. The river flows as it flows, and no law
can prevent it, nor what we hope for, nor the lover we hold
in the deep night—the water makes hardly a sound; it speaks
         all right
but not in a register we can understand or hear, the eternal sound
of things. Silence does not exist, nor will it after our lives,
nor as the planets in their own stately pavane through darkness
and flame. What lasts is our night watch, which we carry.
Which was a kind of rescue, a blending in the mind, not
to become homogeneous, rather a part of the great sound,
the always inexplicable covenant that is made for us,

to enjoy or partake. What are we witnessing as the man
across the street turns on a leaf blower, who would clean,
like some lesser deity, the slowly sifting dust
that will bury us all, like the dust covering Herculaneum,
feet thick, or finding 'Lucy' under all that rock. So much easier
to see time as something actually we could measure,
in human terms, so much better than the tilting rock bursting
but so slowly a man could not even notice and then
we see a twisting mountain before us, crushed and tilted,
layered in stunning colors, each band a monument
to time's irrelevance and the absurdity of measurement.
How long does it take to be dead; how long must we wait
until nothing is meant, the rules altered like the rocks?
Can you imagine them screaming, a geologic fever,
a beauty beyond our ken, but not the less real for that?

Poets claim to desire immortality, lines permanently engraved
in the consciousness of the future. But this is so far beyond,
when our civilization itself is balanced on an arête,
why think of permanence, why think of anything other
than what pleasure is left to be had? Holding the lover near
is probably enough, the miracle of what is, without expectation
or regret. The Exile's seeing, not reduced, in fact expanded,
for our world is little more than a small scale demonstration,
and fortunate as we are to be a part, we cannot let the angels
         of desire
distract us. It is so tempting, and there is so much inner work
         to be done

2)

Learning, if there were a way, a template to follow,
but our gift is quite different. A young friend asked me:

Does it get easier as you grow older? Oh, would it.

Surely comfort is good, but how do you do it?
And to what purpose? Did you ever consider
that circulation might be an answer? Even though we know
nothing comes round again, or if it does,
all has been altered; but to be a contained system,
the heart beating and the seasons changing,
the long whisper of continuance—The spirit calls:
Come back to the world. There is nothing useful
if you have left your body. Even so?
This aged thing no costume can transform.
So what are we to do with our promise, the great dream,
how do we body it, bore through the crust of the earth,
back again into space? We are gathered here,
light years apart; and this is our island.

Being nondescript, that may be the goal. In the middle
of a complex conversation on poetry, George interrupted
by noticing, in the late afternoon light, a last gleam of sunlight
from a window down the hall, gracing a purple glass vase.
How beautiful, he said. And I have forgotten the conversation
completely, but remembered the interruption, over forty
      years later,
which became the real point of it, the gold dust that remained
in the bottom of the pan. Think of it; think of the important times
when something trivial displaced what you thought mattered,
and that now stays with you—we do not know what will
      be important
twenty years from now; we only remember the residue
which was the thing itself, though we didn't know it then.

3)

They had to cut great chunks of the roots
in order to build a smooth, level sidewalk.

I thought the tree might die, or at least
retreat into itself to recover over the next year or two;
but no, it seemed fine; the following year it leafed out as usual,
as though nothing had happened. In the fall, the leaves
reddened later than its neighbor, but were magnificent.
If only we could ignore out wounds, our many limbs grow back,
our roots be cauterized and then continue to explore,
through earth, healthy and whole, a life indestructible.
The dense roots and branches in the back of our property
need to be trimmed in order for the plants to prosper,
allowing the thick cut slabs of Navajo sandstone
to remain seated, a walkway into paradise garden,
hidden among the tangle, secret, as though for children,
who build their world from their freedom, walls
protecting them from the constant tragedy that breaks
like waves, or across a deadly desert, or deeper,
into that underground fort among the black walnut trees,
too bitter to eat the fruit, but lovely to climb, and rest in,
and perhaps read. Just as, under the cabin roof,
drops from the trees, the scamper of squirrels or the hopping
of small birds, all unseen, but recognized, a land
not just for children, but one that belongs to us all,
where dying is the mistaken illusion, where we reach out
to find what we always knew but never realized,
a home where our fading consciousness can rest, and be satisfied.

Strangely, it is easier now to be patient. You'd think,
with the window of our lives beginning to close,
patience would be the last virtue we would practice.

And yet, it is simple to wait, binoculars in hand, for the bird
to turn, show its profile in the afternoon light, reveal itself
so we could name it. Not that the world cares for our naming.
Nature is not indifferent; it cares for something entirely beyond
        our knowing.

Examine a fox's eyes when it stares back at you before it runs.
Whatever connection you discover, it's of a different dimension.
To go there you must discard everything that you thought
        was human.
Like removing your clothes for the first time to a lover,
everything mysterious, and you have no knowledge of what world
you are about to enter. Let us be honest and recognize
that experience is a deception that may allow you to proceed,
but will only blur the actual. You pretend habit as though it
        were a virtue,
you think you know, but her arms that would enfold you
do nothing of the sort, are never repeated, always new.
The love you practice grows like a tree, but it is never the same,
can never be a template. Otherwise your life is a mirage,
a fantasy unachieved, and you will have little choice
but to break the breastbone, dig into the center
among the blood and gristle and lies and indiscretions
to find what you always knew was real, but put away for
        another time.

4)

The cooling air and slanted sun strike away everything familiar.
It is not repetition because there can be no return. So, discouraged,
you find a place to lie down on, a couch, or somewhere
        comfortable
under a tree, or maybe just open under that impossible sky,

and try to understand. Counting the leaves falling, counting
anything that may have a number imbedded, to satisfy,
however unlikely, the mind's craving, the heart's bewilderment.

The swirls in the great trees of the eastern mountains of California,
ancient, to our understanding, present life where little life
        seems possible.

The dead wood awakens, begins a slow dance, a Sarabande.
The wind is steady and cold; the bent shapes are poised to circle,
and strain to the dance, but they remain as though frozen in time.
How is this possible? White dolomite blinding in the scattered sun;
it rains, it hails, it is dark, then brilliant; the trees, spread far apart
talk to each other, through the lightening burns. They don't
        notice us.
We are too far away, our small treading means nothing to them.
And yet, standing there, waiting silently, arms down, mute
and without expectation, there will be a voice; something will
        touch us
so that we turn around to see who it might be, and no one is there,
the quiet trees only. Who is speaking? Who dares interrupt
        the wind?
interrupt the smooth, wind-polished bark, the body of the tree,
endless circles of age, of presence ? But they say we must not
tamp the earth around the base of the trees too much. They
        need space,
the roots need air through the rock. Off to the east are range
        after range
of desert mountains. Alive now, we will become tree,
        become rock,
will transform ourselves without effort or desire. It will
        just happen,
and the trees know this and find their way of welcoming us,
if only we can pay attention.

5)

If all knowledge is gained only through suffering, what is the role
        of joy?
I cannot believe the trees weep from their wounds, or the grass
shudders under our tread. Surely there is a different order
        from pain,

or the regency of pain, temporarily in charge while we
        gaze outwards,
in a thick mist of imprecision. There must be a clearing,
        the location
where the spider hangs outside the window, waiting in
        perfect harmony
for its way of life to continue, the trap set, provision out of
        times' regulation,
the fitting of need, desire, and fulfillment, like a cracked bowl
glued so neatly that you cannot see the join. Feeding is want,
        but more.
But then, where is the home for all things who suffer, whether
        the fox,
his foot caught in the metal trap, or the man who has lost
        everything
he loves, pain of physical torment, the horrifying inventiveness
of our ability to produce agony in others; where does this all fit in?
Is the purring cat dulled by its contentment? Or is the marriage,
long achieved, little more than a compromise, a mutual agreement
of avoidance? Of what really matters? Is ignorance little more
        than 'ignore',
ignoring what we truly know but prefer not to acknowledge? A life
can go on like that endlessly, bumping over the occasional
        rough road,
but never being deterred—extended to the end; goodbye, goodbye,
who are you to say that was not enough?

Animals never ask questions. What can we learn from that?
Animals take the pain as though it were the confluence of rivers.
These are the fountains of Rome, brought, at immense effort,
from the hills so many miles away. We are building aqueducts
into our hearts, that the flow might easily come, transform us,
washed with holy water, a baptism of the colorless, sweet as the
        evening air

and light beyond the Plane trees, an island as its own paradise,
        the owls
just beginning, a dissonant minor 7th, haunting, beautiful,
where darkness paints a swift line between day and heaven.
Watch me. Watch us all. Feel the heat of the day slowly leak out
through the stones, providing a small shelter, an enclosed space,
        protected,
for a time. It is so tempting, to put away your toys, notebook,
        pens, etc.
and follow Hermes, as once suggested—it was yet another
        preliminary effort
to enfold paradise. It gathered pain in a basket, like picking
        blackberries,
to bring home and devour them, one by one, as the marriage
        concluded.

I had wanted to speak here about the twins, knowledge and pain,
but it will not do. It is too simple, elementary perhaps,
but more like the water-walking insects on the quiet stream –
they indent the water, and the explanations we have learned
        are boring.
What religion without dogma can we find to explain anything?

74

They just don't. Each day we must consume new horrors,
        new tragedies.
They pound at us like some musical *hammerschlag.* But then…

One day we were hiking up a mountain stream. It was hot
and the stream was inviting. We saw a small path going down to
        the water,
and followed it to a fine campsite. We took off our clothes and
        jumped in
the glacier cold water. And then I noticed some sort of package on
        a stump
not far away. Got out and found two fresh cucumbers and two
        cleaned,
wrapped trout. It all could have been done only moments before.
How is it we had missed them? We left quickly, trying to catch up
to the other people, but never could. What comic spirit had left
these treasures for us? That evening, up around timberline,
we cooked the trout and ate the cucumber. It was a gift,
        unaccountable.
A friend writes the hardest thing to contemplate is leaving
        this earth,
which must, fairly soon, happen.

But leaving the earth is impossible; it is what we are,
until earth is destroyed by expanding sun, or immense meteor,
or who knows what. And then nothing will have changed, the eyes
of the animals that have no fear will go on. Look closely. In
        the forest,
or the nude mountains of the desert. They are all eyes, seeing us,
seeing everything there is to see, everyone, utterly calm,
        a beatitude
better than rest or even a dance of joy.

6)

Each miracle bends to us, a shaft of sunlight positioned just so,
which we may notice or ignore. Or perhaps not even see.
        The rules here,
as least so far as we may ascertain them, are surely contradictory.
Love is inscrutable in that it finds its home, not as a parasite,
rather as a man wandering alone in the Alabama Hills,
among the great rounded stones where once movies were filmed
but now small seeps nourish a few grasses and flowers,
where one may lie down away from the dirt roads
and California histories, a faint breeze dropping down
from the wall of the Sierra to the west. There is green among
        the rocks;
there is, in this desert landscape more richness than a rain forest.
It grows; its maturity depends on silence. Somewhere out there
is a tiny bleached wooden shack, sturdy enough to repel the
        winter rain
and snow, a single room with a broad view looking east, the
        purple shadows
flecked with shattered sun. No one finds this place. There is a spell
        over it
that makes it invisible to normal eyes. Inside there is faint singing.
A singing of water sliding softly over rounded stones,
harmonies unknown; what once seemed as dissonance
but now is understood as an opening, even as our spaces seem
        restricted,
yet here is the great view down to the valley, the deceptive silence
that is perfect harmony. There is fear, yes, simple fear, like
        the disease
carried by mice under the floorboards, spiders, scorpions, opulent
        dreams of fear,
of being alone, of the wind, inexplicable noises, whatever the mind
        can invent.

Then it is morning and the light begins its gravitational crawl down
      the mountainside,

towards you, you are bathed in light and all terror dissipates
      like smoke,
the ravens walking purposely at your doorstep, croaking, burbling
in the sheer joy of being alive. Oh, there is little time, but time is
      an eternity,
or can be—that is the grain of the wood, the burn of lightening, the
      living rock.

Part 4

Free Falling

Pleasures

These late summer and early autumn afternoons
where I can sit outside in the half-shade and read
are particularly precious. The Anna's Hummingbirds
are calling in their little sawing song; there are chickadees
and titmice and golden-crowned sparrows
with a falling three note call that is almost melancholy.
Chimes ring from a neighbor's yard in the soft breeze.
They ring sometimes in an order exactly like
the first notes of Copland's *Red Pony Suite,*
so, unconsciously, that music, which I complete,
accompanies my reading. Squirrels are busy in the fig tree,
devouring figs that are not ripe enough for me
but fine for them. Mostly though, I look up each time
when I hear the motors of planes, which is often.
I have begun to count them and notice the directions
they come from and fly towards. It is like
when I was a child sitting in the back yard
with a view over the whole San Fernando Valley,
watching airplanes, writing down what kind they were,
whether private or commercial, making games by myself
in the lazy summer afternoons, no one to bother me,
alone with my thoughts and dreams of the future
and the life that spread out endlessly in front of me;
as vast and promising as the entire cream blue sky
above the mountains, and the valley, and my home.

One Morning in San Jose

It is just beginning to get light, a dull grey under low clouds.
I am sitting in a chair, fully awake but eyes closed.
The house is waking as well, creaking and expanding.
Outside a few cars go by on the wet pavement,
and the birds are active along with a chattering
of squirrels in the Live Oaks .Though today
the house is empty, it begins speaking,
muttering about its past, and, if I listen carefully,
the future. People are dim shadows going in and out;
I can hear their dresses swishing on the floors.
They are saying what they would say if the world had ears.
I sit and listen, but am only half attentive.
The road outside is going nowhere, and I am on it,
with no destination in mind, but nonetheless getting there.

The Miracle of Mt. Athos

They were carrying water in large terracotta jugs
up the narrow and dangerous trail.
It was steep, dangerous,
and the sun was almost overpowering.
They didn't complain or talk much—
it was difficult enough just to do
what they had agreed to do.
The sharp rocks offered little purchase.
It was the old story; but why,
why, when when the landscape
was bleached to white, or clear,
did our eyes soak in color?
I mean, have a care, Randall;
your sanity is suspect,
your blood bleeds white
though your shirt is stained red.
Veins and arteries
are only an incomplete picture.
Is it too much to ask for forgiveness?
By now, you are so sick of these questions.
You just want to break out,
allow the eyes to rest, close them if need be,
and begin to swim. After the angels
had set him back, and everyone
had more or less recovered,
the bottles were now placed
near the summit, in a row,
and a crowd began to form.
Turn the water into wine, someone shouted.
The non-drinkers said, *Turn the wine into water.*
Make confusion a rule we can live by.
Behold, nonsense is our credo.
Gib mir Brot. Oh, could it be that easy,
and that painful? A roomful of books

and photographs, a man turning over
the leaves of his life, climbing sometimes,
pausing here, pausing there, understanding
that the past can never return,
but then, neither can it be destroyed.
Relieved, grateful, he went on,
not caring where it all might lead.

Wisdom in the Desert

I had wandered to the trail's junction; one way to an elegant,
      circular return,
but longer than simply turning back the way I had come.
      It was clear
the intelligent thing to do was to turn back. I was already tired,
my health in recovery mode, but nonetheless weakened from
      the cancer.
It would be foolish to do the longer, rock-dense, magnificent
      way back,
and besides, returning the way I came was beautiful, and that,
      after all,
was the point of my walk. I stood there, in the brilliant sun,
      reasoning it out.
Sensible, not foolish. So, of course, I took the longer way. Happily.

Something that Loves Deserts

The shrill Grackles think there is food near me,
that perhaps I will feed them.
It's a long way from the Cancer Ward to here.
Cacti sparkle like obsidian; everything is clean,
washed by sand and wind. The quills
seem almost friendly compared to the knives.
What is under the earth may be beautiful,
but I want sunlight, heat, and dryness.
That other land must wait; it's a dream to distract us from joy.
There is something better ahead, fitting
for a land of creosote bush, and cholla, and saguaro.
I could be happy here, the nourishing liquids dripping into
        me slowly,
the supreme fields of barbed growth almost caressing.
The desert sees my spine-tangled gift, and acknowledges it,
bending in the blinding sun, somnolent and still in the rare
        shadows,
my eyes unaccustomed to this dramatic change, this beauty.

Ground Water

I wanted to speak from the other side,
where the Amargosa slides softly into sand,
then re-emerges some miles further south by the bridge.
How much flows under us, in the desert,
in those deep caverns of our minds.
Like bells ringing where there are no churches,
no citadel of impregnability,
no sweet water where you can kneel down
and dip your hands in it, a Delphic baptism,
in what passes for faith, and is that, truly:
no mistakes in guidance, no accidents, nor tears.
What I wanted was to find out what drove the wind,
what made its silence only disturbed by what it touched.
But silence is not the answer. It is at best a rest stop
on the way, with shade and likeminded friends
stretching their stiff legs and drinking water.
Our minds are not capable to bring happiness
the way horses trot up to us, nuzzle, and are fed at the fence.
Watch their eyes; they glimmer with a knowledge which,
by the strangeness of their tongues, we too can be nourished
and are able to discover this most holy of secrets.
It's not difficult, only demanding.
Let go, I said—to myself, mostly, but really to us all.

Magic Mountain

I had hiked up the steep ridge for hours.
Towards the end of the day, I found myself
on a broad shelf of mostly granite. Peaks all around,
a perfect tarn in the middle, and Lodgepole pine
sparsely surrounding. The water was glass clear,
glacier melt, and completely still. I looked,
but could find no inlet. It must have been fed
underground, which was strange in the high mountains.
And as I looked, no outgoing stream either.
Too cold for swimming but a perfect flat area nearby,
between boulders; so I made my simple camp.
Water from the pond was delicious. The tiny stove
made my freeze=dried stew better
than I thought possible. The few birds quieted,
no rustle anywhere. I looked at the new stars.
Where on earth am I? I wondered,
knowing there was no going back.
I took off my clothes and got into the sleeping bag,
warm after a minute or two. I looked up. I slept.

Pressures

Who drives an ambulance among the trenches,
among bombs and bullets, gathering the dying and the dead?
Who cradles their bodies like angels in the soft evenings?

Who holds the animals? Their eyes recognize the damage we did,
but do not condemn. In time, they become transparent,
spirits touching every leaf, every flower, even the stones eroding.

Who sleeps with us and wishes we had ears?
The war is endless; the Valkyries carry us away,
knowing we are all heroes, all foolish and badly mistaken.

Somewhere there must be a huge room of forgiveness,
but until we can discard everything we believe,
it will seem as though nothing is there,
save an empty field where brambles grow,
and the hard earth is impervious, even to blood.

Spooky

I am living beneath the undertow of time
in an amethyst cave. Above me
the waters sway gently like a summer breeze,
cooling after a hike in the desert
among Mesquite and cholla, and ironwood.
I do not care about time as it doesn't affect me.
The others hurry, but I am here,
stationed as a guard, but one who guards nothing
and simply enjoys the view.
I am living beneath the undertow of time,
and will stay so long as it pleases me.
I answer questions. I am happy.
I wish I could tell you how it is,
among the glittering stones
and water-washed eyes; their clarity
includes every sweet detail of a molten life,
of nature unconcerned even as it changes,
becomes alien to us but not to it.
I wish I could tell you of the trees here,
the singing of finches, mockingbirds, titmice,
and even crows, all in the undertow of time,
and passing, as a magic lantern flickers,
but of a beauty beyond any art, any feeling, any belief.

Golden-Crowned Sparrow

The bird sings only three falling notes, high-pitched,
and a little difficult to hear. I notice them
mostly in Autumn, as the earth cools.
If I'm sitting in my study, I hear them outside,
the song repeated over and over,
a sweet melancholy that makes me wonder
what the inner life, if any, of birds could be.
In the back yard, there are so many wonders to surprise us.
Edward Weston said: a good photographer needs only
to walk back and there will be armfuls of pictures,
all one needs for a lifetime in that small space.
if only we had eyes and hearts to see and hear. But

the Box Elder's leaves are falling, pale green and yellow;
the squirrels chatter and drop unripe figs, partially eaten,
on the flagstone path. Soon hundreds of waxwings will come
in a frenzy to devour the red, ripe pyracantha berries.
They will make a wonderful wheezing noise
along with a wild fluttering of wings.
They will be drunk on the overripe berries.
It will be a celebration, and I hope to be here to watch it.
In a light breeze, small bell chimes ring
from our and the neighbor's yard. The slanted morning light
highlights the leaves and branches, and those faint three notes
from several birds linger in the crisp air.

Free Falling

There are mockingbirds everywhere this morning,
along with the strutting grackles, cactus wrens
and the always annoying house sparrows,
which are not even native. The morning is alive now,
before the heat settles in and slows everything
to the anvil-waves of heat. I am wondering
how I found myself here, in this place,
my veins conduit for herbs and vitamins,
my body being trained to heal itself.
Needing no archaic torso, but needing illness,
needing help, including the conservative woman
at the restaurant to test my conviction.
Knowing I have no guarantees,
no scientific data, no so-called proof.
I am free falling, only certain that this is the right way.
Learning to trust, to have courage as though
I were a young man just beginning, my hand extended,
 accepting the wild world as my guide,
 needing nothing more.

A Metaphysical Poem

Healing is easy; you just follow the protocol.
The only question is: which one?
Wind chimes ring from the neighbor's yard
and our own. If only sound could solve our difficulties.
I am watching the great conveyer belt of time,
upon which I also stand—the sun is so soft
in these late August days, it seems impossible
to let go of desire. Youth and childhood
complement the gentle light and soft breezes.

She stands before me as though the world were wrested away,
replaced beyond dreams, beyond the shadows
of the great desert canyons, an agreed upon tumult
that has stilled. What opens? What is revealed?
What would she tell me if I asked, or could ask plainly,
like a man whose past has gathered together, clumps of elements,
the way the universe is, sticky, matter attracting matter?
A spirit who shovels the past like coal into the burner,
to be consumed but always replenished.

It is like the long drive across the Texas flatlands,
an impossibly black cloud line directly in front.
The giant hailstones will soon begin, incredible noise of the
          pounding hail
all around, no visibility. Follow, a voice said, whatever you do,
do not break the protocol. You will go forward at a walking pace,
find a tin-covered garage. Beneath the fierce racket, they will say
          with awe
how you had just driven under a tornado about to reach
          the ground,
but the miracle is you kept going, you kept following
when that was needed, kept rejecting the dross.

And I thinking all the time—what is the starting point,

93

what is, no, where is the perspective to put it all in order,
until I realize the order is out there but not for me to understand.
Just accept. Begin, kindness to my parents,
kindness to my lovers and friends, a cavalcade of wonders
falling from a cornucopia, oh follow,
lead, bring the healing like the sun, burning, burning,
a fire whose fuel is endless, deep into eternity,
where sickness can have no purchase.

Notes

The Beautiful Changes is also the title of a wonderful Richard Wilbur Poem. I liked it, and the ambiguity of its meaning(s). It seemed to fit this poem.

The Venetian Tower, An English Mystery is a true story, or true myth—not sure which—on the island of Paros, Greece. I lived looking at it every day from my Venetian cottage about 500 feet away. I'm not sure how the Inspector got into the poem, but he won't leave.

Shostakovitch at the Elevator is another true story. For years he was in constant fear they would take him away, or try to.

Fifteen Roads, The Translucent Guides comes from L. Frank Baum's book, *The Road to Oz.* Section 5 refers to *The Lord of the Rings,* in this case the movies which, I must admit, I prefer to the excellent books.

Octets is a group of eight-line poems, inspired by another poet's many six-line poems. I like them very much and decided to do several as well. But somehow, they wanted to have two extra lines, I suppose to complete a kind of mystical Sonnet. *What We're Going to Miss* refers, of course, to hummingbirds.

Desert Songs for the end of Time. Originally, I titled this long poem *Meditations*, which seems to me uninteresting, if more or less accurate. Thinking of Olivier Messiaen's wartime music helped me come up with the present title. Again, the ambiguity of meaning seems appropriate. *Lucy* is the little hominid found in Africa many years ago. George is the great poet, George Oppen, whom I was fortunate enough to know and visit several times. At the end of Section 4, the trees are the Bristlecone pines in the White Mountains of California, thought to be among the oldest living things in the world (some around 5000 years old).

Hammerschlag: see Mahler's 6th Symphony, the finale. In Section 6, the Alabama Hills are to the west of the little town of Lone Pine, California.

The Miracle of Mt. Athos refers to the story of medieval monks climbing the cliffs on a narrow trail. Horrified, the monks saw their servant, carrying water behind them, slip and fall hundreds of feet below to the rocks. Moments later, to their astonishment, they saw the servant again, carrying water as before, with not a drop spilled, up the path. It was said that angels caught him and placed him back on the path. It was for that reason they later built the great monasteries on that mountain, which persist to this day. *Gib mir Brot* refers to a Kathe Kollwitz drawing of a helpless mother while her child begs for bread. I don't know who Randall is.

Spooky refers to an actual monk who does indeed live in an amethyst cave in India (but not underwater). Everything else is my own invention. Or life.

Free Falling: see Rilke's great poem *Archaïscher Torso Apollos (Archaic Torso of Apollo).*

A Metaphysical Poem briefly quotes Yeats' *Among School Children.*

About the Author

Bill Mayer was born and raised in Los Angeles. He received his BA and MA from San Francisco State University, studying with Jack Gilbert, Stan Rice, William Dickey and Nanos Valaoritis. In the late '60s, he was invited to join a poetry workshop with Gilbert, Linda Gregg, Larry Felson, George Stanley, Bill Anderson, Wilbur Wood, and others. The workshop persists to this day with some of its original participants.

Mayer has published 6 books of poetry: *Longing,* (Pangaea, 1992), *The Uncertainty Principle* (*Omnidawn*, 2001), *The Deleted Family* (Paroikia, 2004), *Articulate Matter* (Paroikia, 2012), *A Truce With Fantasy* (Aldrich Press, Kelsay Books, 2015), and now *Free Falling*.

Poems have also appeared in a number of magazines: *Caterpillar, Ironwood, The San Francisco Bay Guardian, Montana Gothic, Five Fingers Review, Red Rock Review, Paris Atlantic Poetry Flash, Alimentum, Danse Macabre,* and *Visions International,* among others. He was included in an anthology of American poets who have lived in Greece, *Kindled Terraces,* edited by Donald Schofield.

Mayer has traveled widely, having spent extended time in Vermont, England, Greece, Hawaii, Monterey, Germany, France, Italy, and Austria. He is also a professional photographer (working with Tony Keppelman on *Hummingbirds,* a photographic essay published by Little-Brown) and an importer of German and Austrian wines. He lives with his wife, Jane McKinne-Mayer, who teaches art history at the California College of the Arts, in Oakland, California.

Kelsay Books

www.ingramcontent.com/pod-product-compliance
Lightning Source LLC
Chambersburg PA
CBHW031000090426
42737CB00007B/611